The Fathers on Celibacy

The Fathers

on

Celibacy

By PETER HARKX

Translation: International Publishing Consultants

ST. NORBERT ABBEY PRESS
De Pere, Wisconsin
U. S. A.
1968

Excerpts from *The Jerusalem Bible,* copyright © 1966 by Darton, Longman & Todd, Ltd. and Doubleday and Company, Inc. Used by permission of the publishers.

Edited by Lisa McGaw

Translated by
Religious Book Consultants

Cover by Patricia Ellen Ricci

© 1968 St. Norbert Abbey Press

270.2
H 8

Standard Book Number 8316-1050-6

Library of Congress Catalog Card Number 69-20287

Printed in the United States of America
ST. NORBERT ABBEY PRESS
De Pere, Wisconsin 54115

CONTENTS

INTRODUCTION

In this study we intend to examine what the Church Fathers have to say concerning the marriage of church ministers. To start with, this statement requires a triple clarification. In the first place it must be noted that here the appellation "Church Father" is not applied only to the individual writers. For our purposes it also embraces the collective activity of ecclesiastical funtionaries from the early days of the Church as recorded in decrees by general or special councils and synods. This does not signify an unfounded interpretation of the term "Church Father" but merely that we shall devote our attention to both their private pronouncements and their collegial activities.

Subsequently it will be noted that the word "celibacy" does not occur very frequently in the text. Celibacy means the unmarried state. In our modern daily usage it is usually linked with the priesthood in the sense of the unmarried state of the priest prescribed by canon law.[1] There is no question of such an obligation in the early Church. There are indeed unmarried ministers, and we can observe a tendency that the clergy should by preference be unmarried. Yet, insofar as this tendency exists, it is still based upon custom which everyone—from the legal point of view—is free to observe or not as he pleases. There is no question yet of a church rule which would regard marriage as an obstacle to being called to the ministry. We find such a legal ruling for the first time at the Council of Bourges in the eleventh century,[2] while the law does not come into force for the whole of the Western Church until the general Council of Lateran in 1123.[3]

Finally: the term "ministers" is rather vague. Who can be deemed to belong to this category? It is possible to be a little more exact by distinguishing between higher and lower ministers or higher and lower ordinations. Yet even then we are left with the question: To whom do these categories refer? The answer will vary according to the time and place under discussion. As a general orientation we may state that wherever we use minister, clergy, church official, and similar terms, it is always the higher minister that is intended. Everywhere and in all cases such higher ministers are considered to be the bishops, priests, and deacons. We shall indicate, wherever necessary, the cases where subdeacons or other church officials are also to be regarded as "higher ordinations."

I.

RELATIONSHIP MINISTRY: MARRIAGE UP TO THE YEAR 350

In the period up to the middle of the fourth century it is impossible to make a clear distinction between the development in East and West. This does not mean that no difference existed: a differently oriented culture, mentality, and way of thought also gives rise to a different approach to questions of theology and canon law. This phenomenon crops up in matters concerning marriage in general and the marriage of ministers in particular. Still, the differing concepts held in the Eastern and Western parts of the Church can up to this time be regarded as multiple points of view concerning the same thing, each with its right of existence. It is only when Constantine transfers the seat of government from Rome to Byzantium in the year 330 that the two parts of the Church begin to diverge more clearly: henceforth the distinction in attitude is more sharply drawn in an atmosphere of mutual rivalry which finally ends in real opposition.

The split is widened by the fact that, from the middle of the fourth century, the Popes begin more deliberately to exercise their authority in actual practice in the Western part of the Church. This state of affairs is facilitated and indeed rendered necessary by the altered circumstances. This means, for our subject, that from this time on, a life of continence becomes generally obligatory for the priest in the West, stimulated and sanctioned by the central authority, while in the East the existing freedom is maintained.

The rules and ideas concerning the marriage of a minister of the Church can be summarized as follows:

1. Higher ecclesiastical functionaries may marry only once; a monogamous marriage is no obstacle to ordination.

2. It seems to be a hallowed custom that ministers should not marry after their ordination; ordination is an impediment to marriage.

3. A growing tendency can be noted for married clergy to live celibate lives; this custom becomes an obligation in the Western church from about 300. Normal married life is regarded in the West as irreconcilable with the ministry.

1. Monogamy

The regulation (decree) that ministers may be

married only once is based upon Paul's express instruction to Timothy and Titus.[4] As the personal ambassadors of the apostle, having full powers, it is their task to organize the churches of Ephesus and Crete. Paul orders them to appoint as leaders of the community men of one wife. In the following chapter we shall examine in more detail the various interpretations given to this text in the fourth century. It is sufficient to note here that around the year 200 the requirement of monogamy was held to be generally binding for bishops and priests. This does not yet mean that this requirement was actually observed everywhere and by everyone. However, from the fact that general opinion at the end of the second century regards this condition as obligatory, we may conclude that a direct link does in fact exist between Paul's command and the aforementioned unanimity; in other words the obligation of the church functionary to remain monogamous is always considered as being of apostolic origin and thus as an unalterable requirement.

So far as the terminology is concerned it must be pointed out that "bigamy" held a different connotation for the Church Fathers than it does for us. In our vocabulary the word refers to the punishable fact of being married to more than one woman at the same time. The church writers of the first centuries, how-

ever, are usually referring to a second marriage after
the death of the first partner; the marriage of a man
to a widow also is often termed "bigamy." In short,
a second marriage, on the part of either the man or
the woman, is considered as bigamy and as such an
impediment to a higher ecclesiastical office.

In his work on monogamy Tertullian (ca. 160-223)
testifies: "Most certainly we are priests, called by
Christ; we are bound to monogamy by virtue of the
ancient law of God (i.e., the Old Testament) which
He proclaimed to us then in his priests."[5] The reference to the Old Testament quoted here deals with
the decree that the high priest "must take a wife in
her virginity" (Lev. 21:13ff.) This text, which in fact
applies only to the high priest, is interpreted by
Tertullian as being applicable to all the priests of
Judaism.[6]

The same author, under the influence of Mon-
tanism, which regarded all that was physical and
material as scarcely or not permissible, even goes so
far as to forge (from the priests' obligation to observe
monogamy) an argument that in fact every Christian
is bound by this law. For do not the other requirements which Paul makes in his instructions to Titus
and Timothy regarding admission to the ministry
apply to normal Christian virtues? Everyone is thus

bound to observe these requirements, but the priests especially must set the example.[7]

Elsewhere in Tertullian we come across the idea that the fact that men who have been married twice are prohibited from occupying a leading function in the Church is a sign that the Church is against second marriages as such.[8] There do indeed seem to be clergy who do not fulfill the stated requirement, but these can be relieved of their function. At least, Tertullian knows of a number of cases in which this has happened.[9]

Another witness to the prohibition which forbids church officials to marry more than once is Hippolytus (ca. 235). This priest of the Church of Rome was involved in a polemic with Pope Callixtus whom he considered too lax and too lenient: "During the time of Callixtus bishops, priests and deacons who had been married twice or even three times began to be admitted to the clergy."[10] We may assume that such cases did in fact occur; we have witnesses of this fact for other times and places. In view of the polemical character of Hippolytus' work we must take with a grain of salt the suggestion that Callixtus tolerated or even actively encouraged this transgression of the law. In any case, however, the statement quoted is a clear indication of the generally accepted opinion that the higher offices of the Church were open only to those who had been married no more than once.

Finally, a letter erroneously ascribed to Pope Stephen I (253-262) also refers to bigamy as an impediment to the higher degrees of ordination.[11]

2. Ordination as an Impediment to Marriage

There are practically no texts which mention a prohibition to marry after a higher ordination. This does not mean that this was an open question, upon which each was free to make a personal decision. The absence of data in this matter indicates not that there was no ruling on the subject but, on the contrary, that the law was so widely known, accepted, and held to be so self-evident that it needed no further mention.

Hippolytus reproaches Callixtus that his laxity has led to members of the clergy marrying even after their ordination: "It even (happens) that a person with a higher degree of ordination who contracts a marriage, continues in his function as though he had not sinned."[12] It is evidently a sanctioned principle that the acceptance of an ecclesiastical office implies a prohibition to marry from this time on.

Canon 1 of the Synod of Neocaesarea (between 314 and 325) lays down that: "a priest who marries must be relieved of his function. If he is guilty of unchastity or adultery he must be excommunicated and—having been relegated to the lay state—do penance."[13] This canon makes a clear distinction: the man who marries after his ordination does something unpermissible which cannot be reconciled with his priestly office; a marriage once contracted is, however, valid and cannot be annulled. The contracting of a marriage is in itself not wrong, but when this is done by a member of the clergy he is offending against the tradition of the Church; it is for this reason that such a person is deprived of his ministry. The case is different when a priest sins against chastity; here the reference is to something which is in itself bad and sinful. Such a person is therefore not only relieved of his function but also comes under the regulations concerning public sinners. Since a member of the clergy cannot be included among the penitents he is first laicized and subsequently excluded from the church community until he has fulfilled the prescribed period of penance.

The rule mentioned here (no marriage after ordination) seems to have been observed from the early days of the Church. When, at the Council of Nicaea (325), a proposal is made that conjugal abstinence should be generally enforced after the higher ordinations, Paphnutius objects to this suggestion; he says that it is sufficient "that those who belong to the clergy should no longer marry, accord-

ing to the ancient tradition of the Church."[14] When
mention is made in the year 325 of an ancient church
tradition we may take it that the tradition in question
is regarded as deriving from the original Christian
community.

The exception which confirms the rule occurs in
Canon 10 of the Synod of Ancyra (314). Here it is
laid down that when, at their ordination, deacons
make a solemn declaration and say that they feel
the need to marry because they cannot remain thus
(celibate), and if they indeed do marry (after their
ordination), they may remain in office because the
bishop has left this possibility open to them. But if
they have remained silent and have accepted by
(receiving) the imposition of hands, to remain in this
state (unmarried) yet nonetheless contract a marriage,
then they lose the diaconate.[15] Here a clear exception
is made for deacons (regarded as the first of the
higher ordinations) and only for them, and even so
it is not unlimited but granted only when they have
expressly stipulated at their ordination that they wish
to retain their freedom. If the bishop nonetheless
accepts them as deacons, he gives them indirect permission to marry eventually. This exception is permitted in order to offer a certain degree of protection
to candidates for the diaconate. For it frequently
occurred that it was not the person himself who

willingly offered himself for ordination, but that the bishop appointed persons who were—sometimes against their will—destined for an ecclesiastical function.

3. Ministry and Continence in Marriage

Is the ministry regarded as reconcilable with the continuance of a normal married life? This question is more important than the two previous points, since priestly celibacy as we know it develops from an obligation to conjugal abstinence if this in fact existed. In general it may be stated that there exists a growing custom for the ministers of the Church to refrain from normal married life. This custom tends to develop into an obligatory rule or at least a sort of social pressure.

Inspired by the high regard in which Christ himself (Matt. 19:12, 27) and St. Paul (1 Cor. 7:32-35; 9:22) held virginity, there were, from the very early days of the Church, men and women who sought to live a more perfect life through virginity or continence in marriage. Athenagoras (ca. 150) desires to hold up as an example to the pagans the exalted nature of Christianity, the inspiration which flows from it and the high moral ideas it believes in; he says, thus, among other things: "There are many to be found among us, both men and women, who remain unmarried their whole life long in the hope of becoming more closely united with God."[16] The same idea is expressed by other apologists of the second century,[17] among whom notably Tertullian: "For how many men and women in the ranks of the Church confess themselves as virgins; they have preferred to bind themselves in loyalty to God, they have restored the honour of their flesh and they have already proclaimed themselves children of the future age by killing in themselves the power of desire and all that has no place in paradise."[18]

It is understandable—and we shall return to this point in Chapter IV—that this general Christian striving for perfection was considered as especially appropriate to the ministers who were, after all, intended to set the example to the flock in everything (1 Pet. 5:3). Did not the apostles, whose successors and imitators the clergy are, set the example on this point? The general feeling among the Church Fathers in any case is that either the apostles were not married or else they left their wives for the sake of Christ. Tertullian quite simply states, by way of a perhaps somewhat premature conclusion: "Since I find nowhere that the other apostles (except Peter) were married, I must of necessity assume that they were either celibate or lived lives of continence."[19] Jerome (342-420) expresses himself a little more cautiously in his polemic against Jovinianus, who regards celibacy or continence in marriage as merely an inducement to acting on the sly: "I go so far with my opponent as to agree that Peter and the other apostles were indeed married, but this was in the time before they had become acquainted with the Gospel. Later when they are made apostles, they renounce married life. . . . In any case, with the exception of the apostle Peter, it is not clear that any of the other apostles were married."[20]

Two circumstances helped to confirm the ideal of virginity after the time of the persecutions, i.e., after 313. The first was the falling away of martyrdom, which throughout the first three centuries had been esteemed as the perfect imitation of Christ. Virginity for Christ's sake now comes to be regarded more seriously as the aspect of permanent self-discipline; it was therefore viewed as a sort of lifelong martyrdom.

A second factor was the abolition of the social obstacles which the Roman law had placed in the way of those who remained unmarried. In the distant past, so that there should never be a shortage of able-bodied men in the empire, a law had been passed imposing various restrictions on unmarried people and childless couples, especially with regard to the law of inheritance. This discriminating law was abolished by Emperor Constantine.[21] This imparted to Christian virginity a sort of social cachet which was also recognized by the state.

Although the ideal of remaining unmarried for Christ's sake persisted strongly, it was not imposed upon ministers as an absolute condition. Paul himself—and there was surely no greater champion of virginity than he—allows the leaders of the Church to marry. For this reason no direct link is made between the ministry and the unmarried state. The trend is, rather, toward marital continence while in office. For the time being this is seen rather as an ideal than a necessary combination.

It is significant that even Tertullian, who was averse to anything that smacked of the physical and in fact considered marriage barely permissible, nowhere states that the clergy should not be allowed to lead normal married lives. From this we may conclude that, at the beginning of the third century, there is as yet no question of a real obligation in this matter.

On the other hand, a custom is growing up, a custom which tends toward the obligatory. This appears from a passage in Clement of Alexandria (ca. 215), who considers it necessary to defend the continuance of normal married life for the clergy. He begins by stating that there can be no conflict between marriage and the service of God; for marriage too is contracted before God. He continues: "But he [Paul] says: 'The unmarried man is anxious about the affairs of the Lord, how to please the Lord, but the married man is anxious about worldly affairs, how to please his wife' (1 Cor. 7:32f.). What can this mean? Is it then not permitted to those who wish to please their wives according to God's will, to give thanks to God? Is the married man not permitted to be concerned about the affairs of God in addition to his marriage? Not at all. But, just as she who is not married is anxious about the affairs of the Lord so that she may be holy in body and spirit, so too is she who is married in the Lord anxious about the interests of her husband and those of God, so that she may be holy in body and spirit. Both are thus holy in the Lord; the one as spouse, the other as virgin." So far we have seen the general arguments in defense of marriage as being equal to virginity; both forms of life can be truly experienced as a service to God. This benevolent attitude toward marriage may stem from the fact that Clement is the first to seek contact with the "world" as consistently and as completely as possible and has a positive appreciation of "temporal" things. A little further on he speaks explicitly of the ministers: "(Paul) for that matter also admits (to office) the man who has been married once; whether a person is a

priest, deacon or layman, he may fulfill his marriage
without reproach; for it is by bringing children into
the world that he will be saved (cf. 1 Tim. 2:15)."[22]

The earliest known decree which made conjugal
abstinence obligatory is that of the Council of Elvira
in Spain, around the year 300. It is a particular Council
so that its decrees are binding only within its own
territory and are thus not valid for the entire Church.
Canon 33 prescribes: "It has pleased (the assembly)
absolutely to forbid bishops, priests and deacons or
all clerics appointed to office to refrain from having
relations with their wives and to produce children;
anyone who does so nonetheless is excluded from
the dignity of the clergy."[23]

The meaning and intention of the decree are clear,
even though, as worded, it expresses exactly the
opposite from what was evidently intended; this
comes through the faulty linguistic procedure of
linking two negative concepts (forbid-refrain). This
prohibition does not come as a complete surprise. One
might stress that it is precisely Elvira which for the
first time makes the discontinuance of normal married
relations a legal obligation, since it is also evident
from other decrees of this same Council, that the
Church of Spain is decidedly rigoristic. In other
words, one could isolate Elvira and give the impression that we are dealing with a somewhat overempha-

sized rightist movement which conforms to the Spanish temperament but which is little suited to other parts of Europe. This impression, however, would not be entirely correct. For, on the one hand, this prohibition is merely setting down what has been practiced for years, while, on the other, similar evidence exists elsewhere of an attempt at codification on this point during this same period.

We have, for example, a synod held at Arles in Gaul and also at the beginning of the fourth century; this assembly of bishops promulgated a decree similar to that of Elvira: "Moreover, we recommend to our brothers—what is right, chaste and honourable—that priests and levites (deacons) should not cohabit with their spouses, since they are preoccupied with their daily work of service. Anyone who acts against this decree must be deprived of his clerical office."[24] Even though the term "recommended" is used, the penal provision against transgression shows clearly that we are here concerned with an obligatory rule.

We would appear justified in regarding this decree of Arles as an adaptation of the ruling of Elvira which is of a similar trend. This seems even more probable in view of the fact that one could quote other examples of Spanish canons which were adopted in southern Gaul. Two points on which the text differs from that of Elvira are to be noted: in the first place the bishops in Arles are not explicitly mentioned as being affected by the prohibition. One might conclude from this that it was considered superfluous to mention bishops, since, in the region in question, there was not one married bishop or at least no bishop who lived as though he were married. Such a conclusion, however, seems to me to be presuming upon the data.

One other special point concerns the wording. While Elvira expressly mentions prohibition, Arles speaks of recommendation; the tone seems somewhat friendlier and milder although we must admit that the threat of punishment is just as strong in both cases. If the difference in tone is indeed of any significance, one might suggest that the Synod was obliged to be more careful with its wording in Gaul, since it was felt either that the clergy was less ready to accept such a ruling than in Spain or that the bishops had less influence to promote it.

There remains yet another possibility to explain the difference: a possibility which is all the more probable since it finds support in the very text of the synodal decree. Elvira is addressed to the subordinate clergy from high to low; there is an authoritative relationship in which rules are laid down for subordinates who are obliged to observe a command or a prohibition. In Arles, on the contrary, the persons addressed are the bishops taking part in the synod; the canon is stated to be addressed to "our brothers" in the episcopate. In other words we are dealing here not with an organ of authority addressing itself to subordinates, but with a deliberation of equals among each other. This interpretation also provides a better explanation of why, in contrast with Elvira, the bishops too are not explicitly mentioned as being subject to the law. So far as practice is concerned, the decree of Arles must be equated with that of Elvira, but whereas the first is more a call to take the same stand, collegially, in a particular matter, the second emphasizes more a ruling which has quite simply been accepted as such.

At the first General Council of Nicaea in 325 it was proposed to make conjugal abstention compulsory for all priests. It may be assumed that the person behind this suggestion was Ossius of Cordoba. As a native of Spain he would have been familiar with what was decided in Elvira twenty years before. He was, moreover, court theologian of Emperor Constantine and, as such, an influential man at this Council, which strongly bears the imprint of the emperor.

The bishops assembled in Nicaea were almost exclusively from the East. The fact that the afore-

mentioned proposal was rejected indicates that even
at this date the Eastern Church possessed a different
outlook on the possibility of reconciling marriage and
ministry. Unfortunately enough we have no evidence
to show whether the Council was unanimous in re-
jecting this suggestion or whether it had the support
at least of a group. Besides, even if we did possess
data concerning the proportion of votes, this would
not mean much since several bishops in Nicaea
showed themselves ready to vote against their con-
victions if they thought that by so doing they could
please Emperor Constantine.

We do know, however, that the proposal was
rejected thanks to the intervention of Paphnutius.[25]
This bishop from Egypt, who was highly esteemed
on account of the tortures he had endured—he had
lost the sight of one eye—and because he lived a
sternly ascetic and celibate life, came into prominence
as the champion of freedom. He suggests three
motives why conjugal abstention should not be made
compulsory for the clergy: (a) marriage is in itself
something good and irreproachable; the proposed
measure might suggest that there was something
reprehensible or, at least, imperfect attached to marriage which would render it irreconcilable with a
position of authority in the Church; (b) the acceptance
of this law would place too heavy a burden upon the

clergy; the majority were, after all, married and were called to office without any suggestion that this would have such far-reaching consequences in the future; (c) the virtue of the priests' wives (abandoned to their fate) would be endangered; what is to become of these women for whom married life is suddenly declared forbidden territory; would they not be tempted to seek elsewhere what they could no longer find in their own homes?

Schillebeeckx links the rejection of the proposal with Encratism; there was the danger that such a rigoristic prohibition would encourage this sect. Encratism was a movement characterized by extreme severity, the rejection of any contact with matter, vegetarianism practiced as a matter of principle, and the denial of marriage. Such, according to the Encratists, must be the normal Christian attitude to life, if they were to be worthy to share in the eternal and definitive Kingdom of Christ, which was close at hand.[26] This factor may perhaps have played a role, but only as a very remote motive. There is no mention of this element in the reports of Paphnutius' activities. The real reason for the rejection of the proposal would seem to have lain, rather, in the different approach to marriage and things physical current in the East, which we have come across before. Otherwise, at a later period when Encratism no longer constituted a danger to the Church, a similar proposal would surely have been made again and accepted.

II

DEVELOPMENT IN THE WEST
FROM 350 ONWARD

1. Monogamy

Generally speaking, the rule of monogamy as a condition of office remains in force, but there is no unanimity concerning the interpretation of the instruction given by Paul to Titus and Timothy. Two problems arise in this connection: (a) is Paul proposing a limiting condition (the holder of office must have been married only once) or a compulsory requirement (the officeholder must be married); (b) does a marriage contracted before baptism count?

a) Toward the end of the fourth century we come across a very remarkable and exceptional interpretation of the words of the apostle which is clearly contrary to the intention of the text. The meaning of Paul's words is clear: he wishes and requires that officeholders should have been married only once. He does not go on to suggest limiting regulations concerning the continuance of normal married life once a person has been received into the ministry.

Nor, evidently, does he say that unmarried people may not be called to office and assume positions of leadership in the community. He proposes a minimum requirement (no more than that) and not a **conditio sine qua non.** And yet in some circles during this period, it is interpreted as a compulsory requirement which must be satisfied: a cleric must be married; admittedly not more than once, but marriage is obligatory.

This divergent opinion was influenced by the activities of Jovinianus, Vigilantius, and other heretics. They went to the opposite extreme from Encratism and came out strongly against asceticism in general and against virginity in particular. They regarded celibacy or conjugal abstinence as an impossible imposition which would inevitably lead to all kinds of excesses and abuses. Taking this idea to its logical conclusion they also denied the virginity of Mary; in their opinion she had several children by Joseph after Jesus' birth. In this way they attacked the ideal of Christian virginity both in itself and in its highest feminine model.

The doctrine that the office-bearer had of necessity to be married, was propagated in the Western Church especially. This is understandable, since the opposite pole of rigorism also found most support in the West. But in the East, too, we see offshoots of this doctrine. In his exposition of the Pauline text in question, John Chrysostom (344-ca. 405) says: "He [the apostle] speaks thus (man with one wife) not in order to state a law according to which (admission to the clergy) would be permissible only under this condition, but to prevent a lack of moderation. . . . But some say that it is required that he should be married."[27]

In the Western Church, Ambrose, in his letter to the community of Vercelle, reacts against the faulty interpretation of Paul's command. In his opinion the marriage limitation imposed by the apostle contains a reference to conjugal abstinence which Ambrose considers obligatory for priests; the text in question, however, is not intended to oblige aspirant priests to marry. "The apostle is a teacher in virtue . . . , who prescribes that (the office-bearer) must be married only once; not in order to exclude the unmarried—for that would exceed the obligation of this rule—but so that he [the office-bearer] should preserve the grace of his baptism through conjugal purity."[28]

Within the framework of his action to persuade the clergy to observe conjugal abstinence, Pope Siricius (384-399) stresses that Paul did not intend, with his rule of monogamy, to exclude the unmarried. "For he who said: 'I wish that all were as I myself am' (unmarried) (1 Cor. 7:7), did not exclude the unmarried."[29]

Finally in this connection there remains to be mentioned Jerome, who strongly opposes bishops who require that a candidate be married before they allow him to be ordained. Without referring explicitly to the text of Paul, he reacts against the doctrine of Vigilantius. In his own distinctive manner, without beating about the bush, he states his case bluntly: "It is scandalous! They say that he [Vigilantius] has bishops as accomplices in his crime, if, that is, one can call them bishops, who refuse to ordain deacons unless they first marry. They think that no unmarried person is capable of chastity; they even hold up their own holy lives as an example, they who think the worst of everyone. They refuse to administer the sacrament of Christ unless they see that the wives of their clergy are pregnant and unless they see children, crowding in their mothers' arms."[30]

b) The opinions held by Jovinianus and Vigilantius may be regarded as extreme, forming part of a body of nonorthodox doctrines. Those who supported these doctrines had already, by so doing, placed themselves outside the Church. But the text of St. Paul contains yet another difficulty, which brings us to the domain of casuistry within the Church and upon which orthodox authors hold different opinions.

The question is this: Does a marriage contracted before baptism, where the wife has since died, count in assessing the once-married status of a cleric? Many answer this question in the negative. Baptism is the beginning of a completely new life in every respect; what has gone before—including an eventual marriage—is a past situation which belongs to another life and thus does not count. A marriage contracted after baptism (provided that it is not with a widow) can claim to be monogamous in the technical sense of the word, even though another marriage already took place before baptism.

This interpretation finds a supporter in Jerome. In a letter to Oceanus, who had cited as an exceptional case the example of a Spanish bishop who had been married before his baptism and had contracted a further marriage after his conversion, Jerome replies: "I am amazed that you should bring up this one example; the whole world is full of ordinations of this sort. And I am not talking now of priests or members of the lower orders; I am thinking of bishops who—if I were to mention them one by one —would form such a large company that it would surpass the numbers of the Synod of Rimini." In the same letter Jerome gives two other reasons why a marriage contracted before conversion does not count. In the first place, when Paul speaks of officeholders, he is naturally referring only to those who are baptized. This being so, the requirements and conditions which he lays down for that office must be viewed from the assumption of baptism. The apostle is not concerned with any situation which may have been present before baptism. Jerome, moreover, detects yet another motive; if one were to follow this argument through consistently one would have to urge that pagans should not marry but give rein to their passions outside marriage; for, should they ever become converted and allow themselves to be baptized, it might appear that—without their desire or knowledge—they had deprived themselves of the right to follow a particular career in life, i.e., in the service of the Church. In other words it is unjust to impose conditions with which a possible candidate could not have complied, since he was ignorant of them.[31]

It seems strange to find Jerome—a fervent champion of the virgin state—taking it upon himself to defend a particular sort of second marriage. Elsewhere he shows that he possesses a different scale of values, according to whether he is dealing with those who have been married once or twice. The former belong to the real Church in the full sense, without spot or wrinkle (Eph. 5:27); the other group belong to a sort of second row of those who call on the name of our Lord (1 Cor. 1:2).[32] It would seem that Jerome here is yielding to the temptation that besets every theologian, namely, that of justifying by argument after the event, an existing phenomenon in the Church.

The apostolic canons, drawn up between 380 and 480, also support the idea that a marriage contracted before baptism does not count. Canon 17 says: "He who has been twice married **after** his baptism . . . cannot become a bishop, priest or deacon or occupy any of the higher ecclesiastical functions."[33]

The opposite viewpoint has among its champions Ambrose, the famous Bishop of Milan (ca. 339-397). Baptism has a bearing only upon sins, which it forgives, and has nothing to do with any legal ties which it supposedly dissolves. He clarifies his thesis, which he regards as a minority opinion, as follows: "Most people are surprised that a second marriage before baptism should constitute an impediment to election to office and the privilege of ordination; for indeed even errors do not usually form an impediment when they are forgiven by the sacrament of baptism. But we must understand that, while guilt can be taken away by baptism, a law cannot be nullified. In marriage there is no question of guilt, but of a legal tie."[34]

Besides the disputed points quoted in connection with the interpretation of Paul's rule, the difficulty still remains of carrying out the requirement and seeing that it is practiced. In his letter to the Church of Vercelli, Ambrose considers it desirable to suggest further arguments in favor of the law of monogamy; he refers in this connection to a decree of the Council of Nicaea—a decree of which nothing further is known. "We know that not only has the apostle laid down this (prohibition of a second marriage) for the bishop and the priest, but that also the Fathers at the Council of Nicaea have added rules to the effect that no one may be a **clericus** who has contracted a second marriage. For how can anyone console a widow, honor her and exhort her to continue in the state of widowhood and in loyalty to her (deceased) husband, if such a person has himself not maintained this loyalty with respect to his first marriage? Or what distinction would there be between people and priest if they were bound by the same laws?"[35]

His argument amounts to this, that the priest must be in all things a model to his flock. He must therefore be seen to possess in his own life that which he holds up to others as an ideal; that which is regarded as desirable for the lay believer must be made obligatory for him. By consistent reasoning Ambrose then arrives at the far-reaching conclusion that the ideal of virginity too must be practiced by the priest, to the extent that he is bound to conjugal abstinence.

The Popes frequently found themselves obliged to emphasize the regulations concerning monogamy for officeholders. In February, 385, Pope Siricius writes to Himerius, Bishop of Tarragona, in Spain, with reference to certain questions which the latter had put to him. One of the questions which the afore-mentioned bishop had submitted to the Pope's judg-ment was: What is to be done with members of the clergy who have been married more than once, for there are several cases in Spain of priests and deacons who find themselves in such circumstances? Siricius sees here more a fault on the part of the bishops who have admitted such persons to ordination than of the candidate himself. He quotes the Old Testament orders of prohibition (Lev. 21:13f.; Ezek. 44:22) and Paul's precept, which he interprets as bind-ing for clerics from the order of deacon. Transgres-sions of this rule occur on such a large scale and "all this is so neglected by the bishops of your region that one might think that the opposite had been laid down." He therefore decrees: Anyone who is now actually in function despite the impediment, owing to ignorance of the prohibition, may continue to exercise his office but may not be promoted to a higher grade; in the future only those who have attained the age of thirty may be ordained deacons; if anybody subsequently breaks the rule of monog-amy, he must be relegated to the lay state.[36]

The Roman synod of January 6, 386, also concerns itself with this matter. Siricius conveys the decrees of the assembly to the bishops of Africa. The reference here is to **clerici** below the rank of deacon: these may if they wish marry again, but they may not marry a widow, and anyone who has married a widow while still a layman may not be admitted to the ranks of the clergy. This indicates thus an extension of Paul's prohibition to cover the lower clergy, an extension, however, which was not everywhere accepted.[37] The **constitutiones apostolicae,** compiled during this period, also express themselves in the most comprehensive terms, i.e., to the effect that no member of the clergy at all is allowed to have been married to a widow.[38]

Popes Innocent I, Celestine I, and Leo I[39] also expound similar views. In a letter to the bishops of Africa, Leo I complains of bigamists in the ministry; there are even some who have remarried after a divorce although the first wife is still alive, or who maintain two wives at the same time; in other words we also hear of cases of bigamy in the customary, strict sense of the word. The Pope demands dismissal from office for all cases of bigamy, whether in what we would call the real sense or not.[40] The same Pope also stresses the condition of monogamy, whereby a marriage contracted before baptism also counts, in pastoral letters to the churches of Italy, Illyria, and Thessalonica.[41]

Pope Hilarius repeats the same ruling in a letter to the Bishop of Tarragona, in which he communicates the decrees of a Roman synod held in November, 465: "Especial care must be taken—as already prescribed in previous decrees—that no one who has married a wife who was not a virgin, aspires to higher ordinations. Those too must be debarred who have contracted a second marriage, contrary to the apostolic directives.[42]

This constant papal activity shows, on the one hand, how anxious the Popes were to preserve the traditional ecclesiastical decrees concerning the clergy. On the other hand, it is clear that the rules were by no means always observed. In May, 594, Gregory I is still advising, that "it should be examined whether a person has perhaps been married twice."[43]

The various papal pronouncements on this point are reflected in the synodal decrees of the particular churches. In the year 441 the Synod of Orange says: "suitable and tested men who have been received into the clerical state on the basis of their good conduct, but who have been married twice cannot occupy any ecclesiastical office higher than the subdiaconate."[44]

The Synod of Arles (524) points out that the rule prohibiting bigamy for bishop, priest, and deacon has been in existence for a long time. The assembly, however, considers it desirable to insist more stringently upon the observance of this rule and lays down punishments for transgression. Any bishop who administers ordination to someone who has been married twice (or to a widow) is suspended for a year; if he nonetheless continues to exercise his functions during this period, complete excommunication follows.[45] It is to be assumed that the bishop has had the candidates' circumstances investigated beforehand.

With the reference to the Council of Braga in Spain, held in the year 563, certain rulings are mentioned which have a bearing upon the matter under discussion. It is laid down that the husband of a widow (and thus certainly someone who has been married twice) may not be admitted to the clergy. It appears from the context that the reference here is to the higher clergy, from the diaconate up. The subdeacon seems to occupy a rather fluctuating position, suspended, as it were, between the higher and lower clergy, but there appears to be a tendency to regard the subdiaconate as a higher ordination. For a lector may marry for the second time, but in this case the highest rank he can hope to achieve—and then only in case of necessity—is that of subdeacon.

If a subdeacon remarries, however, he must step down to the rank of lector. In other words, anyone who remarries may eventually become a subdeacon; but anyone who once holds the office of subdeacon may no longer retain his function if he marries again.[46]

The distinction between higher and lower clergy can vary from place to place. Or it might perhaps be better to say that subjection to the limiting regulations may be extended to cover a greater or less number of ecclesiastical ranks. In certain regions the prohibition with regard to bigamy applies not only to subdeacons but may also include the more subordinate church functionaries. From a testimony given by the bishops of Troyes and Autun in the year 479 it appears that in their dioceses—although not elsewhere—the **ostiarius,** i.e., the lowest grade of the clergy, may not marry for the second time, under penalty of dismissal from office and excommunication. "As regards members of the clergy who marry twice: the Church allows this and tolerates it up to the ostiariate; for the rest every bishop will rightly maintain the rule which he has accepted in his own diocese. Exorcists and subdeacons must be absolutely forbidden to marry for a second time. . . . we no longer permit those who have entered the service of the church, to contract a second marriage. . . . In the church of Autun even an **ostiarius,** who occupies the lowest office, is completely relieved of his function if he takes a second wife. . . . If an exorcist or sub-deacon or even—as we have already mentioned—an **ostiarius,** should be foolish enough to enter upon a second marriage, he is, however, banished not only from office but also from the community."[47]

2. Ordination as an Impediment to Marriage

As we have already mentioned in the previous chapter, it was from the beginning a generally accepted principle that a higher ordination consti-tuted an impediment to marriage. This rule, which was always observed as being self-evident, gave rise to few difficulties even after 350. It is not mentioned, but its existence is assumed.

The lower offices, however, form no impediment to marriage. The apostolic constitutions recognize that "cantors, lectors and **ostiarii** are bound to monog-amy; if they have joined the clergy before marrying, we allow them to take a wife. . . ."[48]

On this point, too, customs may differ according to time and place. At the Council of Hippo in 393 we observe the trend toward a clear-cut position and a uniform practice; this can easily lead to an extension of the marriage prohibition. Canon 22 of the afore-mentioned council rules that lectors who have reached the years of puberty must either marry or take a vow of chastity.[49]

3. Office-holding and Continence in Marriage

In the previous chapter we mentioned particular synods which laid down that the holding of office was irreconcilable with the continuance of married life. However—despite the attempt made by the Council of Nicaea—this did not evolve into a legal obligation valid for the whole of the (Western) Church. On the other hand, the custom becomes increasingly more general that office-holders should lead lives of continence; this attitude is even so widespread that continence in marriage is no longer regarded as an attitude to life which is left to the free choice of the individual. In most places it has acquired an obligatory character, even though this is not always based on an explicit law.

Ambrose, for example, speaks disapprovingly of isolated regions where deacons and priests continue to lead a normal married life on the excuse that they are not in function every day. "You know that the office must be kept pure and spotless and may not be tainted by marital intercourse. . . . I mention this here because in some of the more isolated regions, those who nonetheless exercise the office (of deacon) or even of the priesthood, have fathered children; and they defend this behaviour as based upon an ancient custom, since the sacrifice is offered only once in so many days."[50]

Jerome shows a clear preference for the unmarried priest; he does not wish to exclude married men from office altogether, but they ought in this case to live continent lives. "Christ and Mary, both virgins, have laid the basis of virginity for both sexes. It is for this reason that bishops, priests and deacons are chosen from the ranks of men who have never been married, or who are widowers, or who at least after their ordination live lives of perpetual continence."[51]

Paulinus of Nola (353-431) writes to a priest who was married but who has lived with his wife "as brother and sister" since his ordination, in order to urge him to persevere in this life of continence. "You remain the same spouses as you were before, but not in the same manner. . . . she must attend to temporal matters, so that you are not taken up by them . . . ; a necessary division of tasks whereby she renders unto Caesar the things that are Caesar's, so that you may give to God what is His due."[52]

The still more or less voluntary character of the rulings already mentioned came to an abrupt end when the Popes, with their central authority, ranged themselves behind this custom. The chief initiator of this movement was Pope Siricius; by means of letters to the various churches he attempted to transform into a generally valid church law what up to this time had been merely a pious custom or a local rule.

Himerius, Archbishop of Tarragona, had posed several questions to the Pope, to which the latter replies in a letter dated February, 385: "We have heard that there are several priests of Christ as well as levites (deacons) who, long after their ordination, have begotten children both by their own wives and as the result of unlawful cohabitation; and that they defend their crime by quoting the Old Testament where it is written that priests and levites are allowed to beget children. . . . Why then had the priests in the year of their service to dwell far from their houses in the temple? For this reason, that they might not even have the opportunity to cohabit with their wives, so that with an untroubled conscience they might be able to offer up a sacrifice pleasing to God. Outside the period of their service relations with their wives were permitted only on account of the succession, since according to the law only members of the tribe of Levi were admitted to the service of God. . . . We bind all priests and levites through the imperishable law, that from the day of our ordination we pledge our spirit and our body in the service of sobriety and chastity, if at least we wish to be pleasing to God in all respects in the sacrifices which we offer daily."[53]

In the same document Siricius gives practical directives for the application of the rule: "Since—as your Eminence informs us—there are some who regret that they have erred through ignorance, we are of the opinion that mercy must not be denied them on the condition that they remain in the office which they now fulfill for as long as they live; but they must take care to live henceforth in continence. But those who take refuge in the excuse of an unlawful privilege which according to them is granted them by the old law (the Old Testament) must know that by the authority of the apostolic see they are expelled from every ecclesiastical office which they have used unworthily, and may never more have anything to do with the exalted mysteries of which they have de-prived themselves by their lust for immoral desires. And since existing examples render us all the more alive to the necessity for drawing up precautionary measures for the future (we decree that): every bishop, priest and deacon caught infringing this rule in the future must very well realize that we now exclude him from any possibility of grace; for it is necessary to excise with a knife those wounds which no longer respond to milder means of healing."[54]

On January 6, 386, a synod was held in Rome which, among other things, laid down regulations governing the continuance of married life after admission to the higher ordinations. The decrees of this synod were communicated by Siricius to the Church in Africa. "Moreover we urge—what is just and chaste and pure—that priests and levites should not cohabit with their wives. . . ." This would seem to be no more than a well-intentioned counsel, but it is clear from the rest of the letter that this piece of advice must indeed be interpreted as a binding obligation. "If, in the recklessness of his fleshly desires, anyone should transgress the spirit of this law, he must know that he is to regard himself as banished from our community."[55]

Siricius acts precisely as though he is decreeing nothing new but merely stressing once again an existing law with which everyone is assumed to be familiar. If it were merely a question of the papal letter to Himerius, one might think that he is harking back to the famous decree of the Council of Elvira. A reference to a Spanish regulation, however, would bear little weight with other churches, for example those of Africa. It is more likely therefore that Siricius' measures must not be traced back to any existing, formulated law. On the other hand, the Pope can rightly state that he is introducing nothing new, since conjugal abstinence among the clergy had become practically law by virtue of custom and could thus be generally and officially sanctioned.

Siricius' policy is continued by Pope Innocent I. In reply to questions put by Exuperius of Toulouse and with a reference to Siricius, he repeats the prohibitions and threatened penalties of his predecessor. Nonetheless, Innocent too takes account of the possibility that the regulation in question may not have penetrated to all parts of the Church. In such cases Siricus' rule remains in force, clerics who have transgressed in ignorance may remain in office but lose all chance of promotion. "You ask what must be done with those who—having been appointed to the office of deacon or priest—appear to continue their normal married life or to have begotten children. With regard to these the practice of the divine laws is clear and the unambiguous exhortations of Pope Siricius of blessed memory are sufficiently well-known: anyone holding such office who continues to live a normal married life, must be deprived of every ecclesiastical function and may not be permitted to exercise a work of service which may be fulfilled only in a state of continence. . . . If some appear ignorant of this rule of church life and discipline, which was propagated by Pope Siricius in the various provinces, their ignorance will not be held against them, provided that they live henceforth in continence. They may retain the dignity which they possess, but may not be promoted to a higher rank."[56]

Innocent also communicates the same regulations

to the bishops of Calabria[57] and to Victricius of Rouen.[58]

Pope Leo I also reiterated the same decrees, while introducing two new elements. First, in a letter to Anastasius, Bishop of Thessalonica, he extends the prohibition to include subdeacons. "For while those who are not members of the clergy are free to enter into marriage and to produce children, physical cohabitation can no longer be permitted even to sub-deacons, as an example of the purity of complete continence."[59] He goes on to stress that continence in marriage does not mean that a man must send his wife away. According to some, only complete separation was sufficient guarantee that married life would not be continued. Leo is unwilling to go so far: "the law of conjugal abstinence is the same for servants of the altar (deacons) as for priests and bishops; so long as they remained laymen or lectors they were permitted to marry and to produce children. But when they have attained the above-mentioned offices, that which was hitherto permissible for them is henceforth forbidden. Therefore, so that a spiritual bond may grow from the physical marriage, they may not send their spouses away and must live as though they had none (cf. 1 Cor. 7:29), whereby the love of the married couple remains intact and the conjugal acts cease."[60]

One of the reasons why the Popes begin to insist particularly on the various rules and customs with regard to the marriage of office-holders toward the end of the fourth century—we have already seen how they stressed the rule of monogamy—was the heresy of Vigilantius and his supporters who opposed virginity in general and that of Mary in particular.[61]

Nor is it coincidental that it is precisely the Popes mentioned above who exert themselves most in seeing that the law is carried through and observed; for all three play a special role in strengthening the central power in the Church and in defining more clearly their rights of primacy. Referring to St. Paul (2 Cor. 11:28), Siricius speaks of the anxiety for all the churches which is his responsibility and which gives him the right to intervene and to make arrangements wherever he deems it necessary. Innocent claims the right of appeal with regard to the Western bishops and desires that so-called **causae majores** (important questions) should be submitted to him for decision. The reader is assumed to be familiar with Leo's place in the development of the practice of the primacy.[62]

Leo's rule (continence from the subdiaconate onward, but the wife not to be sent away) remains in force. This appears from letters written by Pope Gregory I toward the end of the sixth century (590-

604). In a missive to the Bishop of Catania he makes it clear that a subdeacon, too, is bound to live in continence; this was not yet the custom there; perhaps on account of the Greek influence in Sicily. "We hear from many sources that you continue to cling to the ancient custom that sub-deacons are permitted married intercourse. By the servant of God, the servant of our see, it is forbidden on the authority of our predecessor that anyone should venture this henceforth and this is to be accomplished in this manner: before the ordination those who are already married must choose between two possibilities: either they must live lives of continence in marriage or else they must renounce the office altogether."[63]

The same Pope exhorts the bishops "to examine what sort of people are being ordained, i.e. it must be noted whether (a future member of the clergy) has lived chastely for several years."[64] On the other hand, it is not the Pope's intention that priests should abandon their wives. The bishops must exhort their priests to live in continence, "but they must add, as the highest juridical power has laid down, that they must not abandon their wives, whom they must guide in chastity."[65]

But for the rest, this life of continence cannot be observed too rigorously. In his **Dialogues** Gregory approvingly quotes the example of a bishop in

Nursia, "who, from the time of his ordination loved his wife as a sister, but was on his guard against her as against an enemy; he never allowed her close to him and under no condition did he permit her to approach him; he had radically put an end to any familiarity between them. . . . lest he should incur the slightest fault on her account he also refused to allow her to perform the necessary services for him." On his deathbed, when his end seemed to have come, his wife touched him to see if he still lived. This was evidently the case, for from the mouth of the dying man sounded: "Depart from me woman, the passion is not yet quenched."[66]

The Synods

One suitable method of seeing how the papal directives were received and put into execution is to examine the reactions of the regional synods in the various districts.

The Church of Africa learned its lesson well: a synod held in Carthage around 390 adopts Siricius' rule and obliges bishops, priests, and deacons to observe the rule of continence.[67] There is admittedly no explicit reference to the Pope's letter to the Church of Africa, which we mentioned earlier, but it seems obvious that an assembly, held shortly after the reception of a papal missive and at which a law is proclaimed similar to that contained in this missive, must have reached its decision under the influence of that document.

The synodal decree of 390 does not yet mean, however, that the clergy immediately adapts itself to the new situation. About a decade later, at a synod in Carthage held in 401, the bishops are still discussing members of the clergy who continue to live as married men. Once again this is forbidden to bishops, priests, and deacons, but now a punitive measure is mentioned: any transgression of the rule will result in dismissal from office. It is explicitly added: "the other (lower) **clerici** are not bound to this continence."[68]

A similar form of regulation has been preserved in the name of a synod said to have been held in Carthage in 419. Here, however, two new elements emerge. In the first place—in imitation of Siricius—the law of conjugal abstinence is seen as a rule which goes back to the apostles: "We too must preserve what the apostles taught and what the early church practiced."[69] The rule, moreover, is now extended to include subdeacons: "Since there have been rumors of the immoderacy of some members of the clergy— even though they be only lectors—with respect to their wives, it is desirable—as has also been laid down by various councils—that subdeacons who are involved in the holy work of service, and also deacons, priests

and bishops, should live lives of continence with
regard to their own spouses according to their own
rules, so that they should appear to be unmarried (cf.
1 Cor. 7:29). If they do not do this they will be
dismissed from their ecclesiastical office. The other
clerici must not be obliged to observe this rule,
unless they have reached the age of maturity.[70]

A decree of the Council of Toledo, held in the
year 400, gives a clear picture of the gradual codification of an existing custom. "Deacons and priests
who have had conjugal relations before the obligation
to abstain was proclaimed by the bishops of Lusi-
tania, cannot be promoted to higher rank."[71] It
appears from this text that the law of conjugal
chastity is of very recent date, yet, on the other hand,
such a coercive custom has evidently existed for so
long on this point that anyone who continues to live
a normal married life—even though no explicit legal
regulations are in force—is considered unworthy of
promotion to the higher ranks of the clergy.

The Synod of Turin held in 401 proposes as
penalty for transgression of the law of conjugal
chastity only the impossibility of promotion; there is
no mention of dismissal from office.[72]

During the course of the fifth century, several
synods were held in Gaul which dealt with the

marriage of the clergy. The Synod of Orange (441) decrees in Canon 22: "It has been decided that in future no married men shall be ordained as deacons, unless they have first promised chastity through their intention to become 'converted.' The conversion mentioned here must be regarded as the taking of a vow of chastity; in this context such an interpretation seems more probable than to understand the term in the sense of becoming a monastic. The text of the Canon quoted may also be read as follows: "It has been decided . . . not to ordain married deacons (as priests). . . ." This is the meaning which Hefele-Leclercq seems to attribute to it.[73] However, bearing in mind the canons which follow immediately afterward, the reference seems clearly to be to the ordination of deacons, not of priests. Canon 23 says in fact: "If anyone who has been ordained a deacon is discovered having conjugal relations with his wife, he is dismissed from office." This is evidently a new ruling for Gaul, for in Canon 24 a transitional rule is made for those who are already deacons: "As regards those who have already been ordained and who continue their normal married life, the sentiments of the Council of Turin must be followed, where it is recommended that they should not be admitted to the higher functions."[74]

The Synod of Arles, held in the year 443, requires an explicit vow of chastity from deacons before they are admitted to ordination as priests. "No married man may be admitted to the priesthood, unless he is first converted (=takes a vow)." [75]

The Synod of Tours held in 461 modifies these requirements somewhat. Priests and deacons are exhorted to observe the rule of chastity, but any transgression is not punished by excommunication; they do, however, lose any possibility of promotion, and transgressors of the law are not permitted to exercise their office.[76]

The combined action of Popes and synods seems not to have been an unqualified success; despite their repeated hammering at the same rule, it remains difficult to ensure that the law is observed. The Synod of Tours even recognizes the necessity for back-pedaling and adopting a somewhat more flexible attitude. In the already quoted letter of Lupus of Troyes and Euphronius of Autun, dating from 479, we even detect a note of defeatism on this point. "It would be better—if this could be achieved—to prevent the begetting of children by those whom we have accepted as married (to the office); but in this case it would be better not to accept married men to wrangle about the subject afterwards in all possible manners; for it is better to prevent every occasion for dispute, so that anyone who does not wish his priests to carry on a normal married life would do better not to appoint married men to the service of the altar."[77]

Synods in the Sixth Century

When a greater degree of flexibility in the rule governing marital relations among the clergy already appeared necessary toward the end of the fifth century, it should come as no surprise to us that this trend continues even more vigorously in the sixth century. This trend is principally connected with the popular migrations. In the first place this is always a troubled period when the normal rules easily lose some of their binding force. Moreover, in many places the priests had fled or been expelled, so that the requirements were somewhat relaxed when it came to selecting new office-bearers. Finally there is another factor which certainly exercised some influence in Gaul and Spain. The Church had to deal with the West Goths who had been converted to (Arian) Christianity from the East by Ulphilas; this Eastern stamp found expression among other things in the priesthood: married priests who continued to live a normal married life.

The Council of Toledo in 589 was obliged to deal with various practical questions. How are West Gothic married priests to be treated if they wish to be converted to orthodoxy? It is easy to say that those who have been brought up in the tradition of married priests should be allowed to retain this

tradition without restriction. But would this not have
an unfavorable influence upon the autochthonous
clergy who are obliged to abstain from marital intercourse? The latter will be easily tempted to follow
the example of the others, all the more so since the
standard has already been lowered. How, on the
other hand, can the leadership, the responsibility,
and the authority of the bishop, which have suffered
considerably under these circumstances, best be
restored or preserved? How can one put an end to
the institution of the **clerici vagantes** produced by
these circumstances, wandering clergymen who at
best offer their services and at worst go about plun-
dering and in any case feel themselves bound by no
authority at all. A council decree had to take all
these facets into account. On the one hand, it had
to be strict enough to restore some order out of
chaos but, on the other, flexible enough to be
acceptable to the well intentioned and to be able to
be put into execution.

Canon 5 of the Council of Toledo gives the following solution: "It has been made known to the
Council that bishops, priests and deacons who have
been converted from the (Arian) heresy, impelled by
physical desire, still continue to cohabit with their
wives. To prevent this happening in the future it is
prescribed as has also been laid down in previous

canons—that they are not to be permitted to continue their cohabitation; but while retaining their conjugal fidelity they must promote their communal interests. They must not continue to share a bedroom or—certainly when virtue demands it—they must send their wives to live in a different house so that chastity may be clearly made manifest before God and before man. If, however, despite this rule, anyone wishes to continue to live with his wife, he must be considered as a lector. With regard to those who have always been subject to the law of the Church: when, contrary to the laws of our forefathers, they permit in their houses the company of women who might make a suspicious impression, they are punished under Canon law and the women themselves are sold by the bishop for the benefit of the poor."[78]

In the canon quoted, a clear distinction is made between those who have been accustomed to a different rule and their own priests who have always been obliged to live lives of continence. Demotion to lector for the first group must not be considered as a punitive measure but as an adaptation of their status within the existing legal framework: lectors, as lower clerics, were permitted to continue their normal married lives.

The Council of Toledo of 589, which we have just mentioned, must be linked with the conversion to Catholicism of the West Gothic King Reccared in 587. As was customary in this case, too, the attitude of the king determined the religious disposition of the people, so that only then does the problem become acute of what is to be done with Arian priests who become converted to orthodoxy. Yet a long way back, in 527, another Council of Toledo had taken measures to keep the quality of their own clergy up to standard.

"Those who are predestined from childhood by their parents to enter the Church, must, immediately after receiving the tonsure or the office of lector, be lodged in a house belonging to the Church where they may be trained under supervision of the bishop. When they have reached the age of eighteen the priest must ask them, in the presence of clergy and people, whether they wish to marry. If, by the grace of God, they choose chastity and take the vow to preserve this chastity, they must, as candidates for the narrow path, be brought under the sweet yoke of the Lord and accept the office of subdeacon in their twentieth year; if they have attained the age of twenty-five without fault or punishment, they must, subject to the approval of the bishop, be promoted to the diaconate. They must remain under supervision so that they do not, contrary to their vow, contract a marriage, or live in concubinage;

should they do so they must be regarded as blas-
phemers and banished from the church community.
But to those who, in reply to the bishop's question,
state that they wish to marry, the permission granted
by the apostle (Paul) may not be refused. If later,
having reached years of maturity, and being married,
they take the vow of chastity with mutual approval,
they may be admitted to the higher ordinations."[79]

For further data we are indebted principally to
various Gallic synods. In Gaul, too, the observance
of the law seems to be in a pretty poor state. The
Synod of Agde in the year 506 recognizes that the
regulations laid down by Siricius and other Popes
have not yet penetrated everywhere. "Should married
deacons and priests wish to continue their married
life, the ruling of Pope Innocent and the decision of
Pope Siricius must be maintained. If this church law
concerning life and way of life which was circulated
by Pope Siricius to the various church provinces,
appears not to have pentrated to some, their ignorance
is not held against them; when they promise to live
chastely in the future they may continue to exercise
the office which they occupy, but they may not be
promoted to higher functions; they must regard it
as a favour that they do not lose the place which they
hold. But those who appear to be acquainted with
the rule of life promulgated by Pope Siricius and

who do not immediately renounce their cupidity must be expelled by all possible means when, having received clear warning, they continue to give preference to their desires."[80]

In order to prevent future transgressions, the same synod sets the minimum age for deacons at twenty-five and for priests and bishops at thirty. In addition future deacons and their wives are required to take the vow of chastity as a condition of ordination.[81] The Synod of Epao in Burgundy (517) also makes a vow of purity a condition of admission to the ranks of the clergy.[82] Since in the latter case there is explicit mention of a transition from layman to cleric, we must assume that Epao requires the lower ranks of the clergy too to observe the rule of continence.

Twenty years later the difficulties are still unresolved. The Synod of Auvergne in the year 535 refuses to beat about the bush and considers it necessary to use strong language. Having laid down in Canon 13 that "every priest and deacon who has received ordination through divine grace, must from that moment become his wife's brother in place of her spouse," those who transgress this rule are charged with maintaining an incestuous relationship. "There are those who, inflamed by the fires of cupidity, have cast aside the girdle of military service (for virtue), have returned to their former vomit, have resumed their forbidden marital intercourse, and have sullied their priesthood by the offence which most properly may be termed incest." Those guilty of this offense are declared deprived of their dignity for ever.[83]

The Synod of Orange, held in the year 538, also considers the bishop responsible. A member of the clergy—in this case from the subdiaconate upward—who has marital relations, is dismissed from office and the bishop who is aware of this fact yet does nothing about it is punished by a three months' suspension. Remarkable enough, marital relations after ordination are regarded as a more grievous offense than an irregular relationship before ordination. Evidently the keeping of a concubine was at that time a fairly common occurrence, which was not felt to be a very serious offense among the people. Canon 9 of the aforementioned synod decrees at least that anyone who has kept a concubine pending marriage or after the death of his wife and has then received an ordination—being ignorant of the fact that this constitutes an impediment to ordination—may still continue to be regarded as a member of the clergy.[84]

In order to prevent transgression of the obligation to observe the rule of chastity, it is repeatedly stressed that members of the clergy must avoid contact with women in general or a least must observe extreme

caution in such contacts. Although there was no
lack of exhortation to this effect in former times, the
second half of the sixth century seems to have been
particularly characterized by too free a social intercourse of clergy with women; even bishops are not
always above suspicion.

In several of his letters, Pope Gregory the Great
refers to the danger to chastity which exists when
members of the clergy persist in regular and solitary
relationships with women, even when these take place
within the framework of their pastoral duties.[85]

When the Council of Tours was held in 567
married bishops still (or again) seem to crop up.
Canon 12, for instance, decrees that: "The bishop
must regard his wife as his sister; wherever he may
be he must always be surrounded by his clergy and
his dwelling must be separate from that of his wife,
so that the members of the clergy who serve the
bishop do not come into contact with the household
servants of the bishop's wife." Here thus we have a
mutual control: the bishop must always be surrounded
by his clergy in order to prevent him from having
unlawful contact with his wife. On the other hand,
the bishop must take care to keep his wife and her
retinue at a distance lest his clergy be led into
temptation. In Canon 13 the clergy are granted the
authority to chase strange women from the bishop's

house. The same synod also pays particular attention to the fate of the clergy in the country. For indeed, if such rigorous measures are already required for the episcopal residence, what then must be the position of the clergy in isolated posts? Canon 19 gives practical directives on this subject: the detailed character of the measures advocated gives us some idea of the actual situation. Archpriests (to be compared with our deacons) must, on pain of a month's penance in default, have someone sleeping in their rooms—even if they are making a tour of visitation; it is proposed that about seven clerics or laymen should perform this duty, turn and turn about. The ordinary priest, deacon, or subdeacon must allow his female servants to live in his wife's house; the aim thus seems to be a complete separation between the cleric and his wife (or any woman). Marital intercourse remains forbidden and is punished by a year's excommunication and permanent dismissal from office.[86]

Various other synods stress the existing regulations.[87]

Conclusion

The rules, valid in the Western Church, are clear:
(a) a second marriage excludes all possibility of office;
(b) marriage is no longer permitted after ordination;
(c) marital relations after ordination are forbidden.

In practice the last law in particular appears difficult to put into execution. True enough, severe punishments await the transgressor, but when the nonobservance of a rule takes on a certain proportion and becomes more or less accepted as normal, sanctions become meaningless.

And yet the Church considers it worthwhile to preserve the law (see the argumentation in Chapter IV). If punishment after the deed proves of no avail, preventive measures must be sought. Possible suggestions include: ordination postponed to a riper age; contacts with women forbidden; have the clergy live together; give an appropriate training from early years (seminary). When even all these measures proved ineffective in certain periods and for certain regions of the Church, finally, in the eleventh or twelfth century, marriage itself was declared an impediment to office. And even so, it was not until the sixteenth century that the celibacy of the priest became the accepted practice in the Church. The fact that only then can the law be put into practice in a more general fashion seems to be attributable to two external factors, i.e., the retention of the law that marriage is an impediment to priesthood, and that a marriage contract entered into after ordination is not only forbidden but also invalid. The second external factor would appear to be the care for the training of priests, stimulated by the Trent seminary decree. Even more important, however, seems to be a third factor which lies not so much in the external plane of practical regulations but which consists in the change in mentality prevalent among clergy and believers thanks to the Catholic Reformation.

III.

THE DEVELOPMENT IN THE
EAST FROM 350 ONWARD

The Eastern Fathers provide considerably fewer texts dealing with the connection between ministry and marriage than do the Western writers. The principal explanation of this difference lies in the fact that the obligation to abstain from marriage which was current in the Western Church and which gave rise there to considerable opposition and numerous difficulties was not laid down in the East, or at least not so absolutely. Without troubling to examine the minor differences which existed between the various Eastern churches we may state as a general rule: in the Eastern churches, too, the tradition is preserved that a second marriage constitutes an impediment to the higher ordinations and that no marriage may be contracted after the (sub) diaconate.[88] The law prohibiting marital relations is accepted in the East only for bishops. This gradually led to the custom of choosing only unmarried men, and notably monks, to fulfill the office of bishop. Nonetheless there are still married bishops in the sixth century;

this appears from the fact that Pope Pelagius (556-561) consecrates a family man as Bishop of Syracuse on the condition that his children will eventually inherit no ecclesiastical property.[89]

1. Monogamy

Although the general rule exists that a second marriage and marriage with a widow constitute grounds for exclusion from office, yet here, too, voices are raised in protest. The Church of Macedonia had pleaded the local custom of admitting to office those who had been married twice. Pope Innocent I rejects this claim: "I have heard that those who have married a widow have not only become **clerici** but have been promoted to the highest rank of the priesthood (the office of bishop); everyone knows that this is contrary to the precepts of the law. No exception on the basis of another law can be made to this rule, supported by divine authority, and this includes the custom which exists among you. The (divergent) rule has, as you yourself say, its origin in ignorance (of the rule); or, to put it more discreetly, is contrary to apostolic tradition and complete insight. You must know that we absolutely refuse to tolerate this in any church of East or West."[90]

Some say that only bigamy in the strict sense (being married to several women at the same time) constitutes an impediment to ordination, but a second marriage after the death of the first wife should not be sufficient reason for exclusion from the ministry. On this point Theodore of Mopsuestia (**ca.** 428) says in his commentary on the Epistle to Timothy: "It is ridiculous that the majority should cling to this interpretation (i.e., that a successive second marriage should be an impediment to ordination); if a respectable man marries a second time, he is not admitted to the ranks of the clergy; yet if a person has been married only once, but misbehaves himself (with another woman) it is debated (whether he may be admitted) even though Paul expressly allows a second marriage, while all cohabitation outside marriage is adultery. . . ."[91]

The same interpretation of bigamy is given by Theodoretus of Cyrrhus (**ca.** 460). [92] From a letter to his colleague in Antioch it appears that it is a frequent custom in Palestine, Antioch, and Berola to elevate men of considerable qualities to the episcopate —even though they have been married for the second time.[93] Since the office of bishop seems open to them, it would appear to be an obvious conclusion that the priesthood and lower functions may be exercised by **bigami.**

2. Ordination as an Impediment to Marriage

In the preceding chapters it has already been stated that the reception of a higher ordination formed an impediment to any further thoughts of marriage. From this one might conclude that those occupying lower positions in the ranks of the clergy were free to marry. A canon of the Council of Chalcedon, however, leads us to suppose that the original ruling was somewhat different, i.e., to enter the ranks of the clergy involves renouncing any idea of marriage. For some reason (perhaps because some of the lower functions were fulfilled by boys of very tender age) in some localities the age at which marriage was no longer permitted was transposed to the higher ordination. In this way what was originally an exception to the rule gradually becomes a generally accepted norm. We feel entitled to conclude this from Canon 14 of the Council of Chalcedon: "Seeing that in some regions lectors and cantors are allowed to marry [this is thus evidently an exception] the holy synod decrees that they are not permitted to marry a woman who is a heretic . . . [the right to marry is, however, recognized]."[94]

Different practices may exist in some separated churches. In 385 a Nestorian synod was held in Persia at which priests were given permission to marry if they so wished; this, however, was rejected by the orthodox churches.[95]

3. Office and Conjugal Abstinence

It would be just as simplistic to imagine that the

Western Church was unanimous in its advocacy of
conjugal abstinence after ordination as it would be
onesided to think that all Eastern writers champion
the continuance of normal married life. In the East,
too, we find defenders and opponents of a continuance
of sexual relations, but, in contrast to the West, the
freer concept here acquires the force of law.

In his history of the Church, Eusebius mentions
Dionysius, Bishop of Corinth (at the end of the second
century) who wrote, among other things, a letter to
the inhabitants of Knosse in which he exhorts Pinynis,
the bishop of that community, not to lay the heavy
burden of continence upon the brothers as an obligation, but to take into account the weakness of the
majority.[96] This intervention on the part of Dionysius
is intended generally to protect all Christians against
encratistic demands; since there is no evidence of a
divergent view with regard to the clergy, we may
assume that they are considered to be on an equal
footing with the rest of the faithful in this respect.

In another work this same Eusebius testifies to an
attempt to introduce conjugal abstinence among the
clergy. "The word of the Scripture says that the
bishop must be a once married man. But those who
are ordained and occupy themselves with the service
of God, ought henceforth to refrain from intercourse
with their wives. But the word of Scripture allows,

even proclaims to all with emphasis, that those who do not consider themselves worthy for the cult must hold marriage in honour and keep married life untainted; for God will judge the immoral and adulterous" (Heb. 13:4).[97]

In his **Symposium,** Methodius of Olympus (second half of the third century) gives a eulogy on virginity; yet no matter how elevated the virgin state, it is not obligatory. Here, too, the ministry is not mentioned, from which we may conclude that for the clergy virginity, though recommended, is not obligatory.[98]

In the fourth century it appears necessary to take action against the exaggerated rigorism of Eustathius of Sebaste, who regarded virginity and conjugal chastity alone as the authentic Christian way of life. The Synod of Gangra in Asia Minor thus emphatically defends marriage in general and that of priests in particular. This latter point finds expression in Canon 4: "If anyone thinks that it is not permissible to participate in the liturgical celebration of a married priest, let him be condemned." The rejection of a onesided ideal of virginity is expressed in Canon 1: "If anyone disapproves of marriage and shows scorn or contempt for an otherwise Christian and pious woman who has relations with her husband, as though she were not worthy to enter the Kingdom (of Heaven)

let him be condemned." This same idea inspires
Canon 9: "If anyone lives a life of virginity or
continence not on account of the exalted and holy
nature of virginity, but out of contempt for marriage,
let him be condemned." In the same spirit Canon 10
declares: "If any one who lives a virgin life for the
Lord's sake, thinks himself better than those who are
married, let him be condemned."[99]

In the fourth century there still seem to have been
a considerable number of bishops who lived as though
they were married. Athanasius (ca. 300-373) testifies
that he knows many bishops who have never been
married, but also many who have children. Viewed
in the context in which a comparison is made between
the lives of monks and of bishops, precisely in their
quality of monastic and highest priest, the reference
would seem to be to children who were born not
before, but during, the episcopate.[100]

Epiphanius, Bishop of Salamis on Cyprus (ca. 315-
403) strikes an entirely different note. He sets out the
practical course to be followed in choosing those who
are to hold office. After a description of the various
forms of Christian life—virginity, the monastic life,
widowerhood, single or multiple marriage—he continues: "The crown and, so to speak, the mother of all
these ranks is the holy priesthood. For this office one
chooses chiefly virgins or otherwise monastics. Or,

should there be no one among the monastics suitable for this office, a person should be selected from among those who lead continent lives or who are widowers of a first marriage. It is not permitted to receive anyone into the priesthood who has been married a second time, even though he lives in continence or is a widower. This holds good for the order of bishop, priest, deacon and subdeacon."[101]

He regards the rule which allows admittance to the priesthood only to those who live celibate or continent lives as a norm which goes back to the apostles.[102] "The matter is thus," he says, "that after Christ's coming on earth the sacred divine law does not admit (to the ministry) those who after a first marriage and the death of their wives, have contracted a second marriage. The reason for this lies in the considerable dignity of the priesthood. The holy Church of God keeps this rule sternly and with the utmost care. Moreover, she does not admit to the office of deacon, priest, bishop or subdeacon anyone—even though he has been married only once—who continues to live a normal married life; she does, however, allow widowers or those who live in continence. This occurs chiefly in places where the laws of the Church are scrupulously observed. But, you will undoubtedly ask me: in some places, priests, deacons and subdeacons have had children nonetheless. This, however, is not in accordance with the rule but proceeds from the remissness of the people who take advantage of the opportunity and on account of the great number (of the faithful), whereas it is impossible to find sufficient ministers.[103]

Here we seem to hear, rather, the testimony of the Western tradition than a representative of the Eastern Church. This might be explained by the fact that Epiphanius is well known for his rigid standpoints and for his often even rash and unmitigated zeal for orthodoxy.[104]

At the end of the fourth century in Egypt the cessation of normal married relations appears customary for a bishop, but not inevitably compulsory. Synesius, Bishop of Ptolemais (400) defends the continuance of his married life: "For, as far as I am concerned, God, the law, and the holy imposition of hands of Theophilus have given me my wife. Well, then, I declare and testify to all, that I shall decidedly not live separated from her, nor live with her stealthily as an adulterer. For the former would show me completely lacking in loyalty to my duty, while the second is in conflict with the normal course of events. But I desire and pray for as many healthy offspring as possible."[105]

The rules may vary from place to place according

to custom. The church historian Socrates (ca. 440) informs us regarding customs in the region of present-day Greece, where continence is obligatory for the clergy. "I am also familiar with another custom in Thessaly; there, if a member of the clergy who has been legally married before, continues to live with his wife after ordination, he is dismissed. In the East, all practice continence voluntarily, including the bishops, without the compulsion of a law which dictates that they must live so. For many of them have had children of a legal marriage, during the time of their episcopate. The person who introduced this custom (of continence) to Thessaly, was Helio-dorus, Bishop of Tricca which is situated there, who—it is said—had composed love poems in his youth and written them in the Ethiopian language. This custom is observed in Thessaly, Macedonia, and Achaia."[106]

Other ideas may be current among the separated churches, as appears from a Nestorian synod dating from the year 499, in which even bishops are allowed to contract a marriage and to continue to have normal marital relations once married.[107]

Sometimes Eastern and Western practices come into conflict with each other. This is the case in Sicily, from early on under Greek jurisdiction but where the Roman practice was introduced shortly before the pontificate of Pope Gregory I. This pope, who made a name for himself as a practical governor and as a realist who takes circumstances into account, gives directives which are adapted to the situation. "Three years ago—as is customary in the Church of Rome—the subdeacons of all the churches of Sicily were forbidden to have relations with their wives. This seems to me burdensome and unfitting, to oblige those who are unfamiliar with the custom of continence and who have not beforehand taken a vow of purity, to part from their wives; and through her absence his fall (in case of sexual intercourse) is all the harder. It therefore seems to me that from today all bishops must be told not to ordain anyone as subdeacon who does not promise to live a life of continence. . . ."[108]

The official—and for the most part still valid—codification of the Eastern customs with regard to marriage and the holding of office, took place at the Trullan Synod, held in Constantinople in 692, at which a stand divergent from the Roman Church was deliberately sanctioned. In Canon 3 various rules were drawn up in connection with a second marriage of clerics: (a) anyone who has married for the second time and has not mended his ways before January, 691, is dismissed from office; (b) anyone who regularizes his position retains his office of priest or deacon, but is not allowed to exercise his function; (c) priests, deacons, and subdeacons who have married a widow or else have contracted a (first) marriage after their ordination may, often doing penance, exercise their function but may not be promoted; in addition, their marriage must be dissolved; (d) in the future no one may become a bishop or even a simple cleric who has contracted a second marriage after baptism or who has married a widow or a woman of suspect morals.

Canon 6 renews the rule that lectors and cantors may marry after ordination, while subdeacons may not. Canon 13: "In the Church of Rome those who wish to receive the diaconate or priesthood promise to have no further relations with their wives. So far as we are concerned, we abide by the apostolic rules and allow continuance of normal married life. Anyone who wishes to dissolve such unions must be dismissed, and the clergyman who abandons his wife on the pretext of a religious motive must be excommunicated. It is agreed however, that subdeacons, deacons, and priests must refrain from conjugal intercourse during the period when they are exercising their sacral functions, for the Council of Carthage has laid down that anyone who performs service in the sanctuary, must be pure."

Finally, Canon 48 decrees that the wife of anyone who becomes a bishop must retire into a convent that is sufficiently far away. The bishop must continue to provide for her. If she is worthy, she can fulfill the office of deaconess.[109]

IV.

MOTIVATION

The link between priesthood and celibacy or continence in marriage is not specifically Christian. Among the Jews the priests were not allowed contact with their wives during the period when they were exercising office. Several of the pagan religions, too, require high standards of purity from those who maintain contact with God in the name of the community. There is a double motive here. On the one hand, an especial love on the part of the divinity cannot be reconciled with affection for a human person; on the other hand, sexuality is regarded as something degrading, influenced by the evil spirit and thus irreconcilable with the purity required for ceremonial worship. It is obvious that the Christians, too, adopted this generally accepted motivation, the distinction being, however, that what in the concept of pagans had to be achieved by one's own power, through ascetism, has, among the Christians, more the character of a charisma granted by God.[110]

Contact with the Sacred

The most frequent motivation for the ideal of

virginity or abstinence from conjugal relations is the contact with God; intimacy with the holy one and with that which is sacred requires that one should refrain from (the practice of) marriage. Speaking of the ideal of virginity in general the apologist Athenagoras already has this to say: "There are many to be found among us, both men and women, who remain unmarried their whole life long in the hope of becoming more closely linked with God."[111] If these motives already play a role for the ordinary Christian, then it is obvious that they will be applied particularly to those who, by virtue of their office, must come into closer contact with God and with the divine. Epiphanius, for example, insists that men who have been married twice may not become priests and that priests should lead lives of continence on account of "the considerable dignity of the priesthood."[112] Pope Leo I will not have it that twice-married men should be chosen as bishops, for "the election to the priesthood is so extraordinary that they are not permitted that which is not accounted culpable among other members of the church."[113]

These few texts serve to show that office-holders, by virtue of their function, are regarded as people of whom higher demands must be made than of other Christians, and these demands touch upon the practice of marriage.

The contact with the sacred is most strongly expressed in the service which the priests have to perform at the altar and in administering the sacraments. Cyprian states that "priests and deacons, who are in the service of the altar and of the sacrifice must be untainted and unblemished."[114] This text deals not with continence in marriage, but with the question of priests who became apostates during the persecutions and who also may not be restored to office after doing penance; in any case, it demonstrates the high requirements demanded by this bishop in connection with the integrity of his priests. The Synod of Arles, held in the year 314, suggests as motive for conjugal abstinence "that they [priests and deacons] are preoccupied by their daily work of service."[115] The **Praecepta Petri,** an apocryphal document dating perhaps from the fifth century, exclude a priest who has had conjugal intercourse from any form of active participation in the holy sacrifice. "If it should happen that, after his ordination, a minister of the altar penetrates the bedchamber of his own wife, he may not set foot in the sanctuary, nor act as intermediary in the sacrifice, nor approach the altar, nor receive the offerings, nor share in the Body of the Lord."[116]

We can expect the clearest and most detailed motivation from Pope Siricius, who was the first to

attempt to introduce the requirement of conjugal
abstinence for all the clergy of the Western Church.
In a letter to the bishops of Africa, he says that
priests and deacons must live in continence "because
they are preoccupied by the daily cares of their
ministry. For Paul wrote to the Corinthians: 'Do not
refuse one another except perhaps by agreement for
a season, that you may devote yourselves to prayer'
(1 Cor. 7:5). If therefore lay people are advised to
abstain from conjugal relations, in order that their
prayers may be heard, how much more necessary is
it for the priest to be ready every minute, protected
by the shield of purity, in case he might have to offer
sacrifice or to baptize."[117]

Some protested against Siricius' measures and
quoted the old covenant whereby priests were permitted to live a normal married life. The Pope
counters that this was necessary at that time in order
to maintain the priesthood, for the office was linked
to the tribe of Levi. But, moreover, even then a
certain degree of conjugal abstinence was prescribed,
notably whenever a priest had active service. In this
connection, Siricius quotes the word of the Scriptures:
" 'Be holy for I, your Lord and God, am also holy'
(Lev. 20:7). Why had the priests during the year of
their service to dwell far from their house in the
temple? For this reason, that they might not even

have the opportunity of living with their wives, so that with an easy conscience they might offer up a sacrifice pleasing to God."[118]

The opponents refused to be silenced: continence may be required when a man serves as a priest. But one does not need to say Mass every day; baptism is not a daily occurrence. The Pope's reply is brief and to the point: ". . . a priest must always be ready to offer up the heavenly sacrifice."[119]

Not only Holy Mass and baptism but also confession are linked with a chaste life. "The Church of Rome particularly observes the following rule: when a person has been baptized as a child and has remained a virgin, he may be admitted to the clergy; also when a person is baptized at a later age and—having married for the first time—lives henceforth a life of continence . . . he too may become a member of the clergy. But anyone who has defiled the water of baptism through sins of the body, even though he has married after his fault, how could such a person share in the office of forgiving sins, when he himself has returned to the blindness of his former life?"[120] Pope Innocent I adopts Siricius' arguments almost literally.[121]

Various synods, too, express themselves in the same spirit. The Synod of Carthage, held in the year

390, makes conjugal abstinence compulsory for bishops, priests, and deacons, "in other words: those who administer the divine sacraments";[122] in 401 the prohibition was extended to subdeacons "who are implicated in the sacred mysteries."[123] The Synod of Auvergne in 535 gives as the motive for the obligation to observe continence that the priests are "elected for the sacred mystery."[124] Finally, the assembly of bishops at Toledo in 633 views continence as a condition "of being worthy to approach the sacrifice of Christ pure in body and spirit and of being able to beg God's forgiveness for the sins of all."[125]

Whenever mention is made of purity as a necessary condition for contact with the sacred, the example is often quoted of David and the holy bread (1 Sam. 21:4-7). Fleeing before Saul, David finds himself obliged to ask the priest Ahimelech for food. The latter, however, has nothing at hand but the holy bread of the Presence, but on David's assurance that neither he nor his young men have had contact with women for several days, he is allowed to take the holy bread. With reference to this story Jerome says: "These holy loaves and the Body of Christ (in the Eucharist) differ from each other as the shadow from the body, as the symbol from reality, as a reference to the future from that which is referred to."[126]

In an address—wrongly attributed to St. Augustine —the rhetorical question is put: "If, for the sake of receiving the holy bread, the priest asks if the servants of David are pure, what then must we poor priests not do in connection with the reception of Christ's body."[127] Veranus of Lyons (at the end of the sixth century) concludes from David's example: "How excellent must he be who approaches the place where the holy mysteries are celebrated in order to plead not only for his own sins but also for those of others."[128]

A special theme which is closely connected with the establishing of contact with God is: the priest must be pure, i.e., live continently in order that his prayers for mankind may more easily and surely be answered. Usually in this connection reference is made to the text of Paul (1 Cor. 7:5) which we have already quoted. This aspect has already been touched upon in our previous chapters, but we also find the same idea expressed in various other texts.[129]

Finally, yet another aspect of the contact with the sacred may be mentioned: the familiarity with the holy Scriptures. On this point Maximus of Turin (ca. 662) writes: "(The priests) like bees gather sweet honey from the flowers of the holy Scriptures. . . . Priests are rightly compared with bees, since, like bees, they preserve physical purity."[130]

Sign of Christ and of the Church

The priest who is a virgin or who lives a life of continence thereby illustrates Christ's virginity and the intact nature of the continuation of Christ which is the Church. Taking as his theme the fact with which they are all familiar, that priests live lives of chastity, Cyril of Jerusalem explains to his catechumens that Christ must have been born of a virgin. "For it is fitting that he, who is the most pure and the teacher of purity, should be born of a virgin marriage. If a person who fulfills the priesthood of Jesus in a fitting manner refrains from relations with his wife, how then could that Jesus himself be born of the co-operation of man and woman?"[131]

Jerome considers the example of Christ as providing the norm for priests. "Christ and Mary, both virgins, laid the basis of virginity for both sexes. The apostles were either celibate or lived lives of continence. It was for this reason thus that men were chosen to be bishops, priests, or deacons who had either never been married, or who were widowers or who at least lived in perpetual abstinence after their ordination."[132]

In his letter to Himerius of Tarragona, Pope Siricius formulates a trinitarian motive for conjugal abstinence. Referring to the Old Testament cultic precepts, he speaks of conjugal abstinence "so that they might, with an easy conscience, offer a sacrifice pleasing to God." A little further on, he continues: [Christ] desired that the radiance of purity should shine out from the Church, whose bridegroom he is (Matt. 5:27), so that on the day of judgment, when he comes again, he shall find her without spot or wrinkle as he instituted her through his apostle (Eph. 5:27). . . . And where could God's Spirit dwell, as we read (Rom. 8:9) but in holy bodies."[133]

This being-like-Christ was chiefly practiced and propagated by the apostles, especially by Paul. Although the latter gives no order, but merely advice (1 Cor. 7:25) he makes no secret of the fact that he would like to see many following this advice. "I wish that all were as I myself am" (1 Cor. 7:7). Thus the association soon comes into being that a true apostolic life ought to include virginity or at least continence. This, too, is why this rule holds good primarily for the successors of the apostles, i.e., the bishops.[134]

Example for the Faithful

A last motive for celibacy or conjugal chastity on the part of the officeholder is of a practical nature: he must practice what he preaches.

In a letter to Pomponius, Cyprian approves his action against the so-called **virgines subintroductae**. By this was understood the abuse that a man who

wished to practice virginity took into his house a
woman with the same ideals. Originally this was
done with the best of intentions, that they should
offer each other mutual support in the common
striving after perfection. But, understandably enough,
the proposed ideal was not always proof against the
difficulties inherent in so close a contact. Pomponius
had therefore forbidden this living together, to the
satisfaction of Cyprian. "For how can (ministers)
take the lead in the matter of chastity and continence
(i.e. control and guidance of virgins) when they themselves set an example of dissipation and vice."[135]

Jerome exhorts: "He who preaches continence
must not counsel marriage. Why does someone, who
has read the words of the apostle: let those who have
wives live as those who have none (1 Cor. 7:29)
compel a virgin to marry? Why does a monogamous
priest exhort a widow to contract a second marriage?"[136]

We find a similar pronouncement in the works of
Siricius: "How dare a bishop or priest have the
effrontery to preach or to counsel continence or
chastity to a widow or a virgin if he himself is more
concerned with producing children for this world
than for God?"[137]

Finally, we may quote the almost proverbial expression attributed to Augustine: **Talis grex, qualis rex.**

"Therefore we, who are called shepherds, must break unchastity by continence . . . ; it is impossible that impure shepherds . . . should make those under them chaste, since the flock is of necessity like the shepherd."[138]

NOTES

1. Cf. R. J. Bunnik, "The Question of Married Priests," **Cross Currents** (1965), p. 407.
2. Conc. Bourges, c. 5 and 6 (in the year 1031): Hef. IV, 953.
3. Conc. Lateranen, c. 7 (in the year 1123): Hef. V, 633.
4. 1 Tim. 3:2 and Titus 1:5f.
5. Tert. de Monogamia 7: PL 2, 939.
6. Tert. **ibid.:** PL 2, 938.
7. Tert. de Monogamia 12: PL 2, 947.
8. Tert. ad. Uxorem I, 7: PL 1, 1286.
9. Tert. de exhort. cast. 7: PL 2, 922.
10. Hippol. philosophoumena IX, 12: PG 16, 3386.
11. Steph. I ep. 1 ad Hilarium: Jaffé 130; PL 3, 1000.
12. Hippol. philosophoumena IX, 12: PG 16, 3386.
13. Syn. Neocaes. c. 1: Hef. I, 327; PL 67, 54 and 155.
14. Socrates hist. eccl. I, 11: PG 67, 101ff. Sozomenus Hist. eccl. I, 23: PG 67, 925.
15. Syn. Ancyra c. 10: Hef. I, 312f.; PL 67, 50ff.
16. Athenagoras suppl. pro Christ. 33: S. Chr. 3, 161; PG 6, 965.
17. Incl. Minucius Felix octavius 31: PL 3, 337; Justinus apol. I, 15: PG 6, 349.
18. Tert. de exhort. cast. 13: PL 2, 930.
19. Tert. de Monogamia 8: PL 2, 939.
20. Hier. adv. Jovinianum I, 26: PL 23, 256.
21. Sozomenus hist. eccl. I, 9: PG 67, 881ff.
22. Clemens Alex. strom. III, 12, 90: PG 8, 1189.
23. Conc. Elvira c. 33: Hef. I, 238f.; PL 84, 305.
24. Syn. Arles c. 6: Hef. I, 295.
25. Hef. I, 620; PG 67, 101ff. and 925; PG 85, 1336f.; PL 21, 473; PL 67, 41f. and 147.

26. Tijdschr. voor theologie 1965, 299.
27. Joh. Chrys. hom. 10 in 1 Tim.: PG 62, 547.
28. Ambr. ep. 63 ad eccl. Vercellensem: PL 16, 1205.
29. Siricius ad episc. Africae: Jaffé 258; PL 13, 1161; PL 56, 729.
30. Hier. adv. Vigilantium 2: PL 23, 355f.
31. Hier. ep. 69 ad Oceanum: PL 22, 653ff.
32. Hier. transl. hom. Origenis in Lucam, hom. 17: PL 26, 259f.
33. Can. apost. 17: PL 67, 143; Hef. I, 1203ff.
34. Ambr. de officiis I, 50: PL 16, 97f.; cf. Ambr. ep. 63 ad eccl. Vercell. 62ff.: PL 16, 1205f.
35. Ambr. ep. 63 ad eccl. Vercell. 64: PL 16, 1206.
36. Siricius ad Himerium: Jaffé 255; PL 13, 1141ff.; PL 56, 560ff. and 860ff.; PL 84, 634ff.
37. Siricius ad episc. Africae: Jaffé 258; PL 13, 1159; PL 56, 728; Hef. II, 70.
38. Const. apost. VI, 17: PG 1, 957.
39. Innoc. ep. 37 Felici Nucerino cap. 2: Jaffé 314; PL 20, 604; PL 67, 249. Innoc. ep. 2 Victricio Rotom. cap. 4-6: Jaffé 286; PL 20, 473ff.; PL 56, 522f.; PL 67, 242f.; PL 84, 646. Coelestinum ad episc. Vienn. et Narbon. cap. 7-8: Jaffé 369; PL 56, 580. Leo ep. 14 Anastasio Thess. cap. 3-4: Jaffé 411; PL 54, 672; PL 67, 293.
40. Leo ep. 12 ad episc. Africanos cap. 5: Jaffé 410: PL 54, 651f. and 661f.
41. Leo ep. 4 episc. Campaniae cap. 2: Jaffé 402; PL 54, 612f.; PL 67, 279. Leo ep. 5 episc. Illyriae cap. 3: Jaffé 403; PL 54, 615f. Leo ep. 6 ad Anastasium Thess. cap. 3: Jaffé 404; PL 54, 618.
42. Hilarius ep. 1 ad episc. Tarrac. cap. 2: Jaffé 560 PL 58, 13; cf. Hef. II, 903.
43. Greg. ep. 4 ad Januarium Caral. cap. 26: Jaffé 1298; PL 77, 695.
44. Conc. Orange c. 25: Hef. II, 446; PL 84, 257.
45. Syn. Arles c. 3: Hef. II, 1062; PL 67, 1090.

46. Syn. Braga c. 26, 43 and 44: Hef. III, 176ff.; PL 84, 578ff.

47. Lupus of Troyes and Euphronius of Autun to Talasius of Angers PL 58, 66ff.

48. Const. apost. VI, 17: PG 1, 957.

49. Conc. Hippo c. 22: Hef. II, 87; cf. PL 56, 425.

50. Ambr. de officiis I, 50: PL 16, 97f.

51. Hier ep. 48 ad Pammachium cap. 21: PL 22, 510.

52. Paulinus ep. 44 to Aprus and Amanda: PL 61, 385-391.

53. Siricius ad Himerium cap. 7-9: Jaffé 255; PL 13, 1138ff.; PL 56, 558f.; PL 84, 633f.

54. **Ibid.**

55. Siricius ep. 5 ad episc. Africae cap. 9: Jaffé 258; PL 13, 1159ff.; PL 56, 728ff.; Hef. II, 71ff.

56. Innoc. ep. 6 Exuperio cap. 1: Jaffé 293; PL 20, 496; PL 56; 501f.; PL 67, 245f.; PL 84, 649f.

57. Innoc. ep. 38 episc. per Brutios: Jaffé 315; PL 20, 605; PL 56, 523f.; PL 67, 243f.

58. Innoc. ep. 2 Victr. Rotom.: Jaffé 286; PL 20, 475ff.; PL 56, 523f.; PL 67, 243f.

59. Leo ep. 14 Anast. Thess. cap. 4: Jaffé 411; PL 54, 672; PL 67, 293.

60. Leo ep. 167 ad Rusticum Narb.: Jaffé 544; PL 54, 1204; PL 84, 766.

61. Schillebeeckx in Tijdschr. voor Theol. 1965, 301f.

62. H. Marot: "The Primacy and Decentralization of the Early Church," **Concilium** (1965), No. 7, p. 5.

63. Greg. ep. lib IV, 36 ad Leonem ep. Catan.: Jaffé 1306; PL 77, 710f.

64. Greg. ep. lib. IV, 26 ad Januarium ep. Caral.: Jaffé 1298; PL 77, 695f.

65. Greg. ep. Lib. IX, 60 ad Romanum: Jaffé 1636; PL 77, 997.

66. Greg dial IV, 11: PL 77, 336f.

67. Syn. Carth. c. 2: Hef. II, 77.

68. Syn. Carth. c. 4: Hef. II, 127; PL 84, 209.

69. PL 56, 864f.; PL 67, 186f.; PL 84, 185.
70. PL 67, 191.
71. Syn. Toledo c. 1: Hef. II, 123; PL 84, 329.
72. Syn. Turin c. 8: Hef. II, 134.
73. Hef. II, 462 nota 2.
74. Conc. Orange c. 22-24: Hef. II, 445f.; PL 84, 257.
75. Syn. Arles c. 2: Hef. II, 462.
76. Syn. Tours c. 1-2: Hef. II, 899.
77. Lupus of Troyes and Euphronius of Autun to Talasius of Angers: PL 58, 66.
78. Syn. Toledo c. 5: Hef. III, 225; PL 54, 352.
79. Syn. Toledo c. 1: Hef. II, 1082f.
80. Syn. Agde c. 9: Hef. II, 985; PL 84, 265.
81. Syn. Agde c. 16-17: Hef. II, 988f.; PL 84, 266.
82. Syn. Epao c. 37: Hef. II, 1041.
83. Syn. Auvergne c. 13: Hef. II, 1141; PL 84, 292f.
84. Syn. Orange c. 2 and 9: Hef. II, 1157ff.; PL 84, 279.
85. Greg. ep. lib. IX, 60 ad Romanum: Jaffé 1636; PL 77, 997; cf. Greg. ep. lib. I, 52 ad Symmachum: Jaffé 1120; PL 77, 515.
86. Syn. Tours c. 12 and 19: Hef. III, 186ff.
87. Syn. Orleans (549) c. 3-4: Hef. III, 159; PL 84, 295. Syn. Macon (583) c. 1, 3 and 11: Hef. III, 202f. Syn. Lyons (583) c. 1: Hef. III, 206. Syn. Auxerre (ca. 586) c. 20-22: Hef. III, 219; PL 72, 765.
88. Const. apost. VI, 17: PG 1, 957.
89. Pelagius ep. Cethego patr.: Jaffé 992; PL 69, 414.
90. Innoc. ep. 17 episc. Maced. cap. 1-2: Jaffé 303; PL 20, 527f.; PL 56, 506f.; PL 84, 665f.
91. Theod. of Mops. comm. in 1 Tim. cap. 3: PG 66, 937ff.
92. Theod. of Cyrrhus comm. in 1 Tim. cap. 3: PG 82, 805.
93. Theod. of Cyrrhus ep. 110 episc. Ant.: PG 83, 1305.
94. Conc. Chalcedon c. 14: Hef. II, 802f.; PL 67, 90 and 174.
95. Hef. II, 930.
96. Eusebius hist. eccl. IV, 23: S. Chr. 31, 204; PG 20, 385ff.
97. Eusebius demonstr. evang. 1, 9: PG 22, 81.

98. Methodius of Olympus symposion or. III, 13: S. Chr. 95, 121f.; PG 18, 82.

99. Syn. Gangra c. 1, 4, 9-10: Hef. I, 1029; PL 67, 58.

100. Athan. ep. ad Dracontium 9: PG 25, 533.

101. Epiph. panarion lib. III, tom. II expos. fidei 21: PG 42, 824.

102. Epiph. panarion lib. II, tom. I haer. 48, 9: PG 41, 868.

103. Epiph. panarion lib. II, tom. I haer. 59, 4: PG 41, 1021ff.

104. Quasten patrology III, 384.

105. Synesius ep. 105 fratri: PG 66, 1485.

106. Socrates hist. eccl. V, 22: PG 67, 637ff.

107. Hef. II, 950f. note 2.

108. Greg. ep. lib. I, 44 ad Petrum subd.: Jaffé 1112; PL 77, 505f.

109. Hef. III, 563ff.

110. Schillebeeckx in Tijdschr. voor Theol. 1965, 306f. (New York: Sheed & Ward).

111. Athenagoras suppl. pro christ. 33: S. Chr. 3, 161; PG 6, 965.

112. Epiph. panarion lib. II, tom. I haer. 59, 4: PG 41, 1024.

113. Leo ep. Anastasio Thessal. cap. 3; Jaffé 411; PL 54, 672; PL 67, 293.

114. Cypr. ep. Stephano papae: PL 3, 1049.

115. Syn. Arles c. 6: Hef. I, 295.

116. Praecepta sancti Petri: PL 56, 895.

117. Siricius ad episc. Africae: Jaffé 258; PL 13, 1160; PL 56, 728; cf. Jef. II, 71.

118. Siricius ad Himerium cap. 8: Jaffé 255; PL 13, 1138; PL 56, 558; pl 84, 633.

119. Siricius ep. 10 ad gallos episc. cap. 2: PL 13, 1186.

120. Ibid. cap. 3: PL 3, 1187.

121. Innoc. Victricio Rotomag. cap. 9: Jaffé 286; PL 20, 476; PL 56, 523f.; PL 67, 243f.

122. Syn. Carth. c. 2: Hef. II, 77 and 202; PL 56, 865; PL 67, 186f.

123. Syn. Carth. c. 4: Hef. II, 127 and 203; PL 67, 191.

124. Syn. Auvergne c. 11: Hef. II, 1141; PL 84, 292.

125. Syn. Toledo c. 21; Hef. III, 270; PL 84, 373.

126. Hier. comm. in ep. ad Titum: PL 26, 569f.

127. Aug. ad fratres in eremo sermo 37: PL 40, 1303.

128. Verani sent. in syn. anno 586: PL 72, 701f.

129. Incl. Hier. comm. in ep. ad Titum: PL 26, 568. Epiph. panarion lib. II, tom. 1 haer. 59, 4: PG 41, 1024. Siricius ad episc. Africae cap. 9: Jaffé 258; PL 13, 1160; P. 56, 728.

130. Maximus of Turin hom. 112: PL 57, 515.

131. Cyril of Jer. catech. 12, 25: PG 33, 757.

132. Hier. ep. 48 ad Pammachium 21: PL 22, 510.

133. Siricius ad Himerium cap. 8: Jaffé 255; PL 13, 113c.; P. 56, 558f.; PL 84, 633f.

134. L. Hödl: Die lex continentiae. Eine problemgeschichtliche Studie über dem Zölibat (Zeitschr. für kath. Theol. 1961, 325-343).

135. Cypr. ep. 62 ad Pomponium: PL 4, 369.

136. Hier. ep. 52 ad Nepotianum 16: PL 22, 539.

137. Siricius ep. 10 ad gallos episc.: PL 13, 1184f.

138. Aug. ad fratres in eremo sermo 42: PL 40, 1316.